Developing a Spiritual Community with Collective Wisdom

Rev. James Yeaw, D.D.
Unity of Fort Collins

Second Edition, 2024
Library of Congress Cataloging-in-Publication Data
Yeaw, James, ed.
Developing a Spiritual Community with Collective Wisdom
 P. cm

ISBN-13: 979-8385670123

1. Church Management

Table of Contents

Chapter 1 – The Future of Churches

There are many questions about the future of churches that have arisen in my conversations with colleagues. In this post-pandemic world, many churches have declined in numbers and in financial support. Their programs have seen a decline, especially those that serve youth and young adults. All generations experience changes, and we're amid a truly radical change, the kind that happens only every few centuries.

Those of us in the West, over age 30, may have been born into a community that could be called "Christian." David Kinnaman at the Barna Group has shown, in America, people who are churchless, that is those having no church affiliation, are about to exceed those that are affiliated with a church or spiritual center. Non-profit donations to religious causes are now less than donations to other types of non-profits. In addition, 48% of Millennials (born between 1984-2002) can be called post-Christian in their beliefs, thinking and worldview.

The change we're seeing around us might be viewed as what happened to the Catholic church after Constantine's conversion or after the invention of the printing press. Whatever the change looks like when it's done, it will be a seismic shift from what we've known. What will the future church be like? And how should we respond? What is likely for the future church?

Every time there is a change in history, there's potential to gain and potential to lose. I believe the potential to gain is greater than the potential to lose. Why?

As despairing or as cynical as some might be over the church's future, we might consider that spirituality will always be here. If the church is a true container for spirituality, it will always continue to exist in one form or another.

The need for spirituality or connection beyond self seems to be hardwired into us. This may be our sixth level of need, the one beyond the other needs, such as physiological needs and safety needs postulated by Abraham Maslow.

Spirituality is a genetically based, physical need that has a metaphysical purpose. It is a natural hunger for supernatural sustenance. It propels us to find meaning and transcend our mundane selves.

Many now believe that spirituality has an evolutionary purpose. This is the thesis of *The God Gene: How Faith Is Hardwired into Our Genes,* by molecular biologist Dean Hamer. "Human spirituality," Hamer says, "has an innate genetic component to it. It doesn't mean that there's one gene that makes people believe in God, but it refers to the fact that humans inherit a predisposition to be spiritual -- to reach out and look for a higher being."

That said, many individual congregations and some entire denominations won't make it. The difference will be between those who cling to a purpose of helping individuals find that fulfillment of spirituality and those who cling to some other model.

Carey Nieuwhof, in his blog on the subject, gives an example. When the car was invented, it quickly took over the horse and buggy. Horse and buggy manufacturers were relegated to boutique status, and many went under, but human transportation exploded. Suddenly average people could travel at a level they never could before. The mission is travel. The model is a buggy, car, or motorcycle, or jet.

Look at the changes in publishing, music and even the photography industry in the last few years. See a trend? The mission is reading. It is music. It is photography. The model always shifts… moving from things like 8 track cassettes and CDs to MP3s and now streaming audio and video. The same can be said of the telephone.

[2]

Companies that show innovation around the mission such as Apple, and Samsung will always beat companies that remain devoted to the method as did Kodak.

Churches need to stay focused on the mission to help people reach out and experience a higher being and a higher truth in their own way. The Millennial generation and future generations will not want to be told what they are to believe. They will want to discover and explore spirituality from a variety of perspectives.

In reading the comments on church leadership blogs, you would think that some believe the best thing to do is to give up on gatherings of any kind. While some will leave, it does not change the fact that the church or spiritual center has always or will always gather because we are also inherently communal. Additionally, what we can do while gathered far surpasses what we can do alone. This is why there will always be a church or spiritually centered gathering of some form. While our gatherings might shift and look different than they do today, we will always gather to do more than we ever could on our own.

Consumer Spirituality will die because it asks the wrong questions. Consumer Religion asks What can we do in the way of programs to attract more people? It asks, what's in it for us, as a church?

That leads us to evaluate our church, our faith, our experience, and each other according to our preferences and whims. In many respects, even many critics of the church who have left did so under the pull of consumer Spirituality because there are not programs to meet their needs. Or they don't like the music. Or they don't feel that are welcomed as part of the community. It is someone else's community.

As the church is reborn, a more authentic, more selfless experience must emerge. Sure, we will still have to make decisions about music, gathering times, but the tone will be different. When we, as a community, must no longer be focused on ourselves and our own viewpoint. A new tone or spirit will emerge.

The death of consumer Religion will change our gatherings. Our gatherings will become less about the "religious" few, such as the Pharisees that Jesus encountered, and more about the spirituality that Jesus and other spiritual teachers expressed. Rather than a gathering of the already-convinced, what will remain will be decidedly outsider-focused. And words will be supplemented with deeds.

In the future church, being right will be less important than doing right. It will be more about how we love than what we know. That involves social justice and meeting physical needs. It also involves treating people with kindness, and compassion in everyday life and attending to their spiritual wellbeing. This is the kind of outward focus that drove the rapid expansion of the first century church. We are cycling back to the essence of those early gatherings.

That's why I'm very excited to be part of a church that has, at its heart, the desire to create a place that unchurched people and people that are spiritual, but not religious, might love to attend. While the expression of what that looks like may change, the intent will not.

Currently, many churches try programs to get people to attend, hoping the programs drive attendance and engagement. In the future, it will flip. The engaged or involved will attend, in large measure because only the engaged will remain. Engagement-driving attendance is exactly what has fueled the church at its best moments throughout history. Engagement is a feeling of belonging, of acceptance, of being loved and being appreciated. That is why Unity of Fort Collins is growing. Through a team approach people are engaged.

For years, the assumption has been that the more a church grew, the more activity it would offer. The challenge, of course, is that church can easily end up burning people out. In some cases, people end up with no life except church life. Some churches offer so many programs for families that families don't even have a chance to be families.

The church at its best has always equipped people to live out their spirituality in the world. But we must be in the world to influence the world. Churches that focus their energies on the few things the church can uniquely do best will emerge as the most effective churches moving forward.

There's a big discussion right now around online church. In certain niches online church might become the church for some who simply have no other access to church.

But there is something about human relationships that requires presence. Because the church at its fullest will always gather, online church will supplement the journey. Online relationships are real relationships, but they are not the greatest relationships people can have. Think of it like meeting someone online. You can have a fantastic relationship. But if you fall in love, you want to meet and spend life together.

There's no question that today online church has become a back door for those who are done with attending church. While online church is an amazing supplement for people who can't get to a service, it's still an off ramp for those whose commitment to spirituality is perhaps less than it might have been at an earlier point.

Within a few years, the dust will settle and a new role for online church will emerge. Online church has the potential to become a front door for the curious, the unconvinced and for those who want to know what spirituality is about.

In the same way we purchase almost nothing without reading online reviews or rarely visit a restaurant without checking it out online first, a church's online presence will be a first home for people which for many, will lead to a personal connection and ultimately the gathered church.

At the same time, churches will also establish smaller, more intimate gatherings as millennials and others seek tighter connections and groups. Paradoxically, future large churches will likely become large not because they necessarily gather thousands in one space, but because they gather thousands through dozens of smaller gatherings under some form of shared leadership. Some of those gatherings might be as simple as at a coffee shop or even home venues under a simpler structure.

James Trapp, the spiritual leader at Spiritual Life Center in Sacramento also gives us a key ingredient in spirituality of the future: He states that one of his teachers posed the question, "If Jesus was seated at a table with a Buddhist, a Hindu, a Muslim, a Zoroastrian and a Shintoist, do you think he would turn to them and say, 'You must all forsake your beliefs and accept Christianity?'".

It is a good question to ponder.

I'm confident that Jesus would not take such a position since he taught spiritual principles that anyone, regardless of what path they have chosen, or if they have no spiritual path at all, can apply in their life.

Dr. Trapp believes there are many paths to understanding this presence we call God. One of the greatest values that he got from traveling to other countries – particularly Ghana and Nigeria- has been the opportunity to understand how others have used their traditions to deepen their understanding of the nature of God, the nature of humanity, and how the two are connected.

At the bottom line, most people seek to understand their purpose in life, how to make a positive difference in their communities, and how to be a more loving presence in our world. Indeed, regardless of background, culture, or religion, we are more alike than different.

Dr. Trapp states that a major challenge we face in our world is that many have bought into the belief of separation. This belief breeds a sense of isolation and an "us versus them" mentality that often leads to behavior that reinforces this sense of separation. As a result, many who do have an active prayer practice tend to only pray for their friends. Jesus challenged this when he said, "Pray for your enemies".

Of course, he was not saying to not pray for our friends, he was saying expand our point of view and begin to bring into daily practice people that we may not like, who may not agree with us, or seem to have an opposite point of view.
As we begin to reach out in an inward way, we challenge the perception of isolation, and we expand our purview of what a neighbor is. Then we begin to discover, as Jesus said, that the so-called enemy is in our own household, probably our own self.

So, in practicing spirituality, we expand our prayer practice and consciously embrace any individual or group of people – past, present or future – we may have been at odds with so as to break through any sense of separation. This one strategy will help anchor the "Beloved Community," the church of the future, which is a Divine Idea in the mind of God.

When we practice principles such as these, we break down the artificial barriers we have created between people, groups, and nations. We begin to look at each other and we will begin to see beauty and not differences. We will begin to say things like "Look at that wonderful light shining through that person." We'll not see color, rather we'll see the different shades of the Infinite. We'll not just see different cultures or religions; we'll see how Infinite Spirit needs all cultures and religions to reveal its unlimited nature. We also need to include all faith traditions, all shades of those traditions, so that our centers of spirituality become centers of collective wisdom.

Change is happening on a macro level in our world, but also on a micro level – one conversation at a time, one group at a time, one church at a time, one new idea spawned among a group of committed people, setting off a chain reaction of new possibilities for spirituality. This reminds me of the words of Margaret Mead who stated: Never doubt that a small group of thoughtful, committed citizens can change the world; indeed, it's the only thing that ever has. Likewise, I believe this kind of transformation not only is possible but has always been the way change happens. Transformation always has a personal dimension and each individual matters. Transformation involves a fundamental shift in our thinking, and an understanding of collective wisdom.

Our capacity for collective wisdom is innate and its emergence in groups is catalyzed by awareness of a compelling need and a higher purpose. Amid the crises we face there is an opportunity to seek fresh perspectives. These perspectives are clear when we look at economic crises; global climate change; immigration; hunger; global conflicts; and the future of spirituality.

The science of collective wisdom is a practice that resonates with the Millennial, Generation Z, and Gen Alpha. It is what resonates with the emerging culture. It is what arises out of spirituality where we recognize the inherent Divinity of each individual. It takes down patriarchy, matriarchy, and all manner of superior power structures. It recognizes the abilities and creativity that is unleashed when we work cooperatively in unison with each other, envisioning the answers to the questions we face today and in the coming decades.

Chapter 2 – The Fort Collins Experience

On August 24, 2020, the Council of Unity of Fort Collins participated in an afternoon retreat. The subject was to be a review and a decision about moving forward after a difficult two years. The difficulty not only was in the two-year pandemic with their closed buildings, but in the recent release of a minister after only a short time of employment. The release was because "there wasn't a good match."

Unity of Fort Collins had never, in recent history, had a Unity-ordained minister. The succession of ministers included individuals that served in a pastoral role but had never been given firm direction of roles in the ministry. The church was and is self-run by a council and various individuals that fill key roles. A small cadre of heartfelt and heart-motivated individuals cared for their spiritual home. There wasn't much use for denominational experts. Plans or programs that were viewed as coming down from the "mother ship," as Unity Worldwide Ministries is sometimes called, were avoided. In fact, the community withdrew itself from Unity Worldwide at some time in the past, but Unity Worldwide didn't even know it.

Self-sufficient! Self-running! Independent! A mixture of theologies and thought! That was and still is Unity of Fort Collins. The council was elected by the members that are all self-declaring, wasn't even the go-to or the in-charge body because anyone could attend a meeting – a sort of mini-community meeting – and they all voted! This obviously was a problem for a Unity-minister-to-be as she was going through field training to be ordained.

The question before our council in August of 2020 was that there were several models for governing and managing a spiritual community. They decided to look at four or five and see which one they fit into.

Minister-centric, board centric, self-governing teams and other choices were discussed. That discussion quickly

Team Diagram

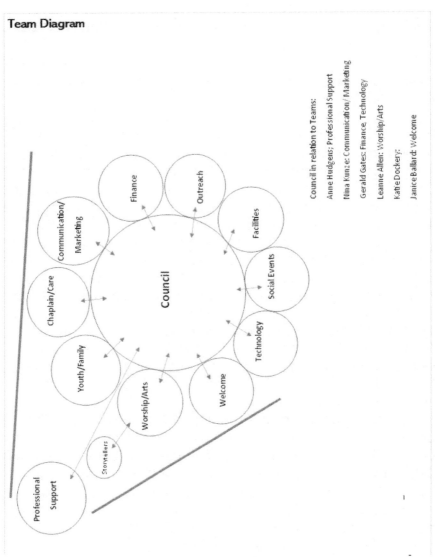

Council in relation to Teams:

Anne Hudgens: Professional Support

Nina Kunze: Communication/Marketing

Gerald Gates: Finance Technology

Leanne Allen: Worship/Arts

Katie Dockery:

Janice Ballard: Welcome

turned to the team approach. With more than 30 or 40 tasks readily identified, the group divided the tasks and decided on teams that would be self-governing. The teams would have their own structure. They would have their own responsibilities. They would not depend on the council except in two areas: expenditures outside the budget and

[10]

activities that did not fit into the vision and values of Unity of Fort Collins.

Each team would select its own leaders and would recruit its own members. The idea was not new to this community because there were several already functioning, although informal, teams in operation.

The plan was introduced to the congregation. More than 70 individuals stepped up to populate the program. The teams, with more than two years of experience, continue to operate successfully, busily engaged in their own corner of the life of the ministry. Again, engagement is the secret to growth and commitment to a ministry.

Several interesting situations have arisen. One example was the Welcoming Team. It welcomes, greets, and sees that visitors and infrequent attenders are assimilated into the community. This team realized that these "newbies" were unfamiliar with the layout of the buildings. They took it upon themselves, to plan, to fund, and to obtain interior signage to direct individuals to the Rumi Room, the Fillmore Room, or the Welcome Room. Then they decided that those being welcomed did not know where the bookstore was tucked away in the church office. They moved the bookstore to a new public place and have staffed it on Sunday mornings. There was a perceived need and they filled it! And they consulted with the Facilities Team to ensure an agreeable working relationship.

The Council previously designated tithes to worthwhile non-profit organizations. This happened without a deep vetting of the organization. With many tasks on their plate, this task was previously just suggested on the fly by those in the meeting of the council. The new Outreach team took on the task and incorporated it on a menu of outreach projects that ranged from Christmas toys for the needy to an outreach project in Guatemala.

The Connections Team surveyed the congregation on activities the congregation was interested in a woman's group, hikes, potlucks...

The Support/Service team is noteworthy in that it is made up of the ministers, the president of the Council and the church administrator. Meeting in person weekly, it supports teams and plans the services and a variety of classes.

These teams manage their specialized tasks, sending a monthly written report to the council. They work cooperatively but independently from the council, ministers, or staff. The council, ministers and staff support their efforts as coaches, encouragers, and resource people. The center of decision making is with the teams as long as they are within the approved budget and their projects or decisions are within the values and vision of the church.

Specifically, what does the council and the ministers do?[1] The scope of the ministerial tasks include speaking at half of the weekly services plus the special seasonal services; teaching of some of the classes; pastoral support; and the coaching of the teams.

At least twice monthly the presenter is a member of the congregation or a person from Fort Collins, often from another faith tradition. We have found that these presentations have several beneficial results. It provides a variety of practical spiritual lessons from various members of the congregation. As individuals long on a spiritual path, share from their experience, including difficulties, it is clear that others do not feel as alone. Spiritual maturity is often expected from a spiritual leader, but the sharing of another "just like me" has proven to be inspiring and makes a strong connection or bond within the community.

The community has also invited others, including Muslim Imams, Jewish Rabbis, followers of Yogananda, to

---

[1] See Appendices I and II

share their spiritual wisdom. Those that are convinced that they cannot be the speaker for a longer lesson are invited to share a reading, a poem, or a thought within the service.

The music is also a team presentation. The community has attracted two professional musicians to share the position of music director. These musicians share the weekly services in planning the music. Those in the congregation with musical talent are encouraged to be part of the service. Presenters and musicians work with the Support/Service team (council liaison, ministers, church administrator) to provide a continuity from week-to-week.

The council approves budgets, ensures legal compliance, and furthers the mission of the ministry.

How does this fit into collective wisdom as discussed later in this book?

Most churches are administered by a comparatively small group of individuals, typically less than a dozen. In a team-centered church, at least five or six times this number actively participate in collective wisdom.

In most ministries there are deeply ingrained traditions. While many of these traditions continue, the inclusion of many individuals means that Unity of Fort Collins is able to include diverse perspectives and passionately welcome most all that is arising. The diversity hopefully, over time, will attract the friends and acquaintances of those that have direct participation and ownership of the ministry. This is the engagement referred to in the last chapter that leads to growth.

We previously referenced the Welcoming Team as to how it operates as a small group. There is an evolving set of close relationships and social interaction outside the work of the team. While "the work" seems to be the purpose, there are several side benefits. Actually, the primary benefit, or the primary purpose, is to draw people together and incorporate those that are new or recent into the life of the community. As we get to know individuals the Welcoming Team introduces them to a team and encourages them to be involved socially and functionally.

There are always challenges. As the structure improves, we will be able to strengthen all teams so that they work in compassionate small groups and where all voices are heard. We carefully encourage one or two to not dominate the leadership. We are able to fully incorporate the principles of collective wisdom, explained in the next chapters, into decisions. We are able to free the council to be discerners of the future instead of guardians of the past. We are able to have the dozens of volunteers relax into a trust of transcendent wisdom, a deep welcoming of all that is arising, and a release of any protective fear as to where this weird[2] ministry is heading. There is still work to be done and work that will continue as we have experienced growth in numbers, in community, and in spiritual emphasis.

---

[2] We often refer to ourselves as a weird church based on my early Sunday lesson by that title. This was based on a book, *Weird Church, Welcome to the 21st Century* by Paul Nixon and Beth Estock.

Chapter 3 – Spiritual Precepts

Now that we have explored the philosophy behind the team approach to management and governance of a ministry, it is important to share the foundational spiritual precepts that lie beneath all the activity and community connections that have arisen. It is easy to overlook the spiritual purpose and the Unity teachings when we share individual spiritual paths and interfaith or interspiritual messages.

Without attention to spiritual percepts, we may drift into dualism, a negation of our own divinity, or a prayer practice based on lack instead of affirming the good that flows within the community. Therefore, as we explain the basics of teams operating together in ministry, we remind ourselves of our spiritual underpinnings and mention how they influence the team approach.

First of all, we know that there is only one presence and one power. With our community, some call that presence "God" while others may prefer another name, such as "Source." In "that" we live and move and have our being.

That "Source" is of infinite ability, infinite potential, infinite goodness, infinite intelligence, and infinite wisdom. We draw on all those attributes and more in every thought, action, or consideration in the ministry. And all of us, regardless of any training or experience, embody those same attributes. Each individual, active in the ministry, or not, is a divine presence. Our spiritual leaders or our elected leaders do not have any greater portion of those attributes than any other individual affiliated with our community.

In keeping with this truth of this individual and collective egalitarianism, we do not label or classify those that choose to be part of our community by a level of activity, nor exclude them because of a membership requirement. All who choose to be part of our community are fully embraced without requirement. We do not use classes taken, certificates earned, length of time affiliated, volunteer time given, nor contributions made as a measure of their loving acceptance of oneness with us.

Likewise, we keep in mind that we are a diverse community even in areas where there does not seem to yet be the desired diversity and inclusion. Our teams keep D&I (Diversity and Inclusion) as part of our awareness. If we do not practice D&I, we will not attract those diverse community members nor be already practiced in inclusion when they enter our doors.

Jesus of Nazareth is one of many master teachers that have blessed our understanding. While many of us endeavor to understand and make his words our credo, others among us may embrace the words of other master teachers as their spiritual path. We accept and celebrate that freedom. Our teams are observant to the various paths of those in our community in all that we do.

In prayer we pray from the realization that prayer is a way that we affirm our good and manifest what we desire and which is ready to manifest. We pray from affirmations of gratitude, not from need or want as we engage in our team meetings.

While we are a Unity Center focused on the foundational teachings of Charles and Myrtle Fillmore; The Fillmores centered their writings on the teachings of Jesus of Nazareth as recorded in the Gospels, both canonical and those not included in the Christian Bible.

The heart of our Unity center is the recognition that there are many approaches to the spiritual journey. We don't advocate for a rejection of individual traditions or for the creation of a new super-spirituality. A favorite saying is the Hindu aphorism: "The paths are many, but the goal is the same." Hence, we are all of that, and our community is free to explore all of that. We are, therefore. Interspiritual.

The term 'interspirituality' was coined by Wayne Teasdale, author of *The Mystic Heart: Discovering a*

Universal Spirituality in the World's Religions.[3] He believed that spirituality is at the heart of all the world religions. He also used the terms "global spirituality" and 'interspiritual wisdom'. He writes that since mystical spirituality is the origin of all the world's religions, this shared spiritual heritage enables us to go beyond differences in theological beliefs and traditions. We are asked if we abandoned Christianity; are we encouraging others to do the same in favor of a single new religion? Our reply is "By no means!"

First of all, interspiritual is not meant to be the mixing of the various traditions but the possibility that we can learn and be nourished from more than our own mystical tradition. It also suggests that there is universal metaphysics from which all particular religions are derived.

As Episcopal priest, author and retreat leader, Cynthia Bourgault puts it: *Wisdom is an ancient tradition, not limited to one particular religious expression but are the headwaters of all the great sacred paths.*[4]

Huston Smith, the preeminent authority on world religions, actually practiced Hindu Vedanta, Zen Buddhism, and Sufi Islam for more than ten years each—while remaining a member of his local Methodist Church. He was deeply interested in knowing how that worked. How could he remain a Christian while exploring and even accepting aspects of other religious traditions? He was asked: "Why are you still a Christian?" His answer was "Christianity is the string on which I hang my beads."

At Unity of Fort Collins, we have a tradition that is "InterSpiritual Wisdom: Sharing the Mystic Heart." We have had presenters from Buddhism, Christianity, Hinduism, Islam/Sufism and Judaism, who talked about their own spiritual beliefs and practices. At times another element

---

[3] Teasdale, Wayne. *The Mystic Heart: Discovering a Universal Spirituality in the World's Religions.* Novato, CA: New World Library, 1999, page 27

[4] Bourgeault, Cynthia, *The Wisdom Way of Knowing: Reclaiming an Ancient Tradition to Awaken the Heart.* San Francisco: Jossey-Bass, 2003, page 4.

could be that they teach a practice to us. Each segment could be followed by a period of meditation when we could practice on our own. The evaluations we received so far from attendees overwhelmingly indicate that they want more of the same.

It seems like interspirituality might be tapping into a need that our churches have been unwittingly neglecting. It's a perspective that may appeal to those more attracted to mysticism than to a dogmatic faith belief; one of the interests of the "nones" that have dropped church as important in life. It also removes the difficulties of an interfaith theology and reframes the conversation in terms of an interfaith spirituality. It does not address, nor does it claim to address, the issues of differences within the traditions.[5]

These precepts underpin our team efforts as does collective wisdom, deep listening, a suspension of certainty, seeking of group discernment and a welcoming of all that is arising. These are explained in the following chapters. Before we look at these topics, we introduce Quaker practices as an example.

Chapter 4 - Practicing the Quaker Way

When a group gathers to make a decision, one of three processes is usually used: the autocratic, the democratic, or the consensus decision-making process. Quakers, especially in their meetings for business, use a fourth process: the Quaker way.

This way is fundamentally different from the other three. Some techniques of the Quaker way are similar to the consensus process, a process that was or is used by Unity of Fort Collins. But, as Howard Brinton pointed out in *Reaching Decisions: The Quaker Method*[6], the Quaker way differs radically in that it is spiritual. George Fox was quite clear about the unique nature of the Quaker way. Fox wrote, "Friends are not to meet like a company of people about town or parish business…but to wait upon the Lord." We would like to work with the Quaker process and incorporate it more fully over time. We believe it contributes to the way of peace in the world in which we live.

The greatest importance has to be that this decision-making process will enable us to discern the Spirit's will for the ministry or team. This discernment leaves the participants changed, empowered to do our work in the world.

The basis of the Quaker way is the belief that a group of persons can discern Spirit's direction. D. Elton Trueblood wrote in *Beyond Dilemmas*[7] that the immense belief of Quakers in the reality of continued revelation makes them expect a revelation of Spirit's will in a group meeting. "They accordingly arranged a group meeting in a manner best calculated to know that revelation…"

Unity is the result of finding Spirit's direction for the group. Spirit leads us in unity. Howard Brinton explained that

---

[6] Brinton, Howard *Reaching Decisions: The Quaker Method* Pendle Hill Publications 2014
[7] Trueblood, D. Elton *Beyond Dilemmas* Impact Books, 1979

since there is but one Light and one Truth, if the Light be faithfully followed, unity will result. He stated that the nearer the members of a group come to this one Light, the nearer they will be to one another, "as the spokes of a wheel approach each other as they near the center."

The following six essentials is a description of the actual process involved in the Quaker way of reaching group decisions.

1. Silence—The Quaker decision-making process takes place in a context of silence. Silence opens and closes the meeting and can be woven throughout. It is employed during the meeting to enable thoughtful listening and prayerful consideration to occur.

2. Presentation of the business agenda.

3. Discussion—Ideas and thoughts are spoken by all who have information or opinions regarding it. In the discussion, the participants seek information, attempting to see Spirit's direction arising from any side of an issue. Differences are recognized, accepted and worked through to an understanding of them and/or to creative solutions to them.

4. Sense of the meeting—In reaching decisions, participants seek divine guidance within themselves and in one another. When the consideration reaches a stage where a reasonable degree of unity has been reached, the moderator announces what is believed to be the sense of the meeting. The group decision is identified by a statement which all agree expresses the sense.

5. Writing the minute—A statement is placed in written form, called a "minute." This may be modified, but once accepted, it becomes the judgment of the meeting and is preserved in the records.

6. Response to serious differences— When serious differences of opinion exist, the group may search for unity through silence, followed by further discussion. When the meeting cannot achieve unity on a subject, the subject is

either dropped or postponed ("held over"). If a decision cannot be postponed and a serious difference of opinion exists, the decision may be left to a small committee.

Unity does not mean unanimity. A person may find that they are not in unity with the sense of the meeting. In such a case, at least three alternatives are available to the individual. The person may agree to stand aside, having expressed a contrary opinion but seeing that the group has clearly reached a sense of the meeting. A more serious stand is to ask to be recorded as opposed.

In this situation the person's objection is noted, although the group is still able to proceed with its decision. The most serious alternative is for an individual to be unwilling for the meeting to proceed. In this situation, the moderator usually has to determine the seriousness of the individual' objection. If the objection is determined to be frivolous, the moderator may state that the sense of the meeting is in another direction and proceed with the meeting. If the objection is a serious one, the group will delay its decision on the issue. The time gained by the delay can be used constructively to enable all the participants to reconsider their positions through thought and prayer as well as to listen to and "labor with" the objection. The original issue then becomes an item of business at a succeeding meeting.

Three conditions especially favorable to the success of the Quaker way are:

1.   The participants bring to the meeting a common understanding of, a faith in, a commitment to the way.

2.   A community and commonality exist among the group participants; and

3.   The participants bring helpful skills and abilities to the group.

The first is the most important. Any decision-making group needs participants who share the belief that

Truth/Spirit's will/a right way/Spirit's leading exists on any given issue and can be discovered by a loving, patient, persistent, open search. Another helpful shared belief is in the worth of waiting, that is, enabling the group to stop short of a decision until the next meeting to allow individuals time to seek within themselves or with one another. What if each participant came to the meeting committed to finding Spirit's solution for the group and willing, in most cases, to set aside opinions and desires in favor of that? The group also needs the shared belief in the Spirit-directed life, in the continued revelation of Truth—through oneself and any other participant. Such understanding, beliefs, and commitments shared by the participants provide the basis for the group search for Spirit's direction.

Individuals in any Quaker group will be aided in their work if they know one another. According to Howard Brinton, "The Quaker method is likely to be successful in proportion as the members are acquainted with one another, better still if real affection exists among them." Groups improve their decision-making abilities as they increase and deepen their community-building activities within their meetings. Small group discussions, prayer groups, fellowship times, shared meals, and workdays are important ingredients to creating community.

In many ways, teams and meetings of those teams are the crucibles of communities. Participation in such a group requires us to be open to change, open to one another, and open to Spirit. Can we disagree and love at the same time? Can we go beyond our initial misunderstandings of one another? Can we get past our judgments of others and appreciate their insights? We can, if real affection exists among us.

The third condition especially favorable to success consists of the participants' skills and abilities. Each participant is essential to the team or the group's search. The participants' ability to open themselves to the Spirit's leadings, is one of the most important abilities to bring to the group. The abilities to listen, to be patient, and to speak audibly and gently are very helpful. Dealing constructively with conflict and being imaginative in the search for solutions are other helpful skills. The ability to gracefully withdraw objections and to help others accomplish this is important.

Constructive use of humor is a real gift to any group.

Spirit-filled facilitating abilities can greatly encourage meetings. The ability to submerge the group in silence, to call for silent searching, to gain participation by all, to clarify the issues, and to keep the discussion on track are extremely helpful.

Our goal is to search for divine guidance for the group, to find it, and to embrace it. To accomplish this, we need to use many of our capacities. All of our human abilities should be used to help each member of the group to understand each issue, to listen to one another, and to be patient with the process. All of our divine/human capacities should be used to open ourselves to Spirit's direction.

Individual meditation is good preparation. Full participation in the "centering" opening silence period melds us into the group's search for Spirit's will. When each of us holds the group "in the Light" while we participate, the group's spiritual awareness is increased.

Listening for Spirit's guidance expressed within ourselves and from any other member of the group keeps us truly attentive. Looking for the creative alternative, "the way through" confusion and conflict helps us recognize Spirit working among us. Expecting Spirit's direction for the group prepares us to find and to embrace divine leaders.

Spirit's guidance has been experienced by teams or groups in at least three ways: through silence, through statements by individuals, and through the group's discovery of a "new way."

Michael Sheeran has given a great gift by his presentation of "real life" 20th-century reports of some of these holy occasions. In his book *Beyond Majority Rule: Voteless Decisions in the Religious Society of Friends.*[8]

In 1948, there were 750,000 refugees on the Gaza Strip; the new state of Israel had just been established. The United Nations asked American Friends Service Committee to take responsibility for feeding, housing, and other services. At the meeting of the AFSC Board of Directors, all speakers said the work needed doing, but all agreed it was just too big for the Service Committee. They counseled us that we should say no, with regrets.

Then the chairman called for a period of silence, prayer, meditation. Ten or fifteen minutes went by in which no one spoke. The chairman opened the discussion once again. The view around the table was completely changed: "Of course, we have to do it." There was complete unity.

Another report by Sheeran describes the way in which one person's statement brought a previously divided meeting into unity. Sheeran feels this case illustrates a number of factors common to such a situation. In his words: "The group feared disunity, and was attempting to conduct itself in a prayerful, even a gathered atmosphere. The speaker himself felt moved to speak. The speaker's remarks were so deeply consistent with the atmosphere of united, reverent searching that he seemed to speak in a divinely authenticated way."

Spirit also works through the group discovery of a new way. This occurs in instances where the group's result is greater than the sum of the parts. A new way opens after much struggling together, and the solution is different from and superior to anything any individual had so far offered. Bit by bit, a new way, Spirit's way, is found. Unity would benefit from more reports of occasions when Spirit's will be discerned by a group. Descriptions of how the leading came and how it was recognized provide a basis for future

---

[8] Sheeran, Michael *Beyond Majority Rule: Voteless Decisions in the Religious Society of Friends* Philadelphia Yearly Meeting of Religious Society of Friends, 1983

discoveries. This process forms the basis of what we call collective wisdom.

Chapter 5 – Collective Wisdom

So, what is collective wisdom? Those that have experienced it tell us that one of the qualities is a sense of connection with one another and to a transcendent presence. Often these experiences are grounded in the understanding of the sacred, however that is defined by members of the group. Carol Frenier was interviewed by Craig Hamilton about her experience with the phenomenon. She observed:

> "In these group experiences people have access to a kind of knowing that's bigger than what we normally experience with each other... You feel the presence of the sacred and you sense that everybody in the group is also feeling that.

> Those who talk about their experiences of collective wisdom often report a sense of openness and awareness of something larger than themselves. There is an ability to communicate that seems broader, and people are often astounded by the creativity that comes forward. "You have a sense," Frenier observed, "that the whole group is creating together, and you don't exactly know how.[9]"

This experience of connection, when it arises, often expands, or dissipates our experience of boundaries – between the team members and the group and others outside the group. Also, between what is personal and what is universal. In another interview conducted by Hamilton, a woman observed: "In the group, I experienced a

---

[9] Hamilton, Craig. Come Together: The Mystery of Collective Intelligence," What is Enlightenment? Issue 25 (May-July 2004)

kind of consciousness that was almost singularity, like a dropping of personalities and joining together where there was no sense of conflict. Nobody was in opposition, and everybody was just helping each other. It became obvious that we weren't responding to individual personalities but were responding to something much deeper, much more real in each other that was collective, something that we shared – a commonality, a reality."[10]

These are words like that shared by members of our Welcoming Team, especially Camina Sylvestro and Courtney Fuchs, at Unity of Fort Collins. They have shared an amazing account of a team working together fostering creativity. This arose as they joined together cooperatively in their decision making and project creation.

Experiences of connection almost feel mystical, almost magical. But they are also quite natural. Meg Wheatley is quoted in *The World Café: Shaping our Futures Through Conversations that Matter*.[11] She stated that the wisdom we possess is unavailable to all of us as individuals. The wisdom emerges as we get more and more connected with each other. We carry ideas from conversation to conversation. We also carry those ideas from one conversation to another.

She states that there is a good scientific explanation for this, because that is how life works. As separate personalities and their ideas become connected to each other; emergence arises. Emergence is the appearance of new possibilities, greater capabilities, and deeper intelligence. The whole becomes more than the sum of its parts. All living systems work in that way. We get confused and we lose sight of this remarkable process where

[10] Ibid
[11] Brown, Juanita *The World Café: Shaping Our Futures Through Conversations That Matter* (San Francisco: Berrett-Koehler Publications)

individual thought and action, when connected, lead to much greater capacity.

Wheatley has another surprising point when she states that collective wisdom feels magical, extraordinary, and often unreal because we have become so focused on the rational. Our minds have become shrunk by detailed analysis, a paralysis by analysis. We have lost touch with the ways that a new capacity and collective intelligence has always come into being. We have reinforced the perception that collective wisdom is only available to the few, the initiated, or the great teachers of our faith traditions. We have given up finding it and actualizing it within ourselves.

Collective wisdom is available and is the potential of all groups. This is not some declaration of naïve faith or a wistful prayer. Collective wisdom is available to all groups because, as Wheatley writes, this is how life works. Intelligence is present in all life forms, and it expands exponentially as we join with others in exploring ideas and common problems. While this is a truth, collective wisdom arises when a certain set of circumstances are present.

These circumstances are:
- Deep Listening
- A Suspension of Certainty
- A Seeking of Diverse Perspectives
- Group Discernment
- A Welcoming of all that is Arising.
- Trust in the Transcendent

We are exploring these topics in subsequent chapters.

Chapter 6 – Deep Listening

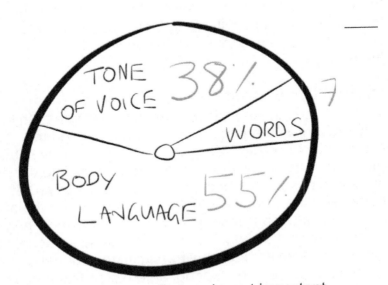

Deep listening is our first and most important practice in realizing the power of collective wisdom.

There is a lot going on during a conversation. The speaker must put into words not just information but often complex perceptions, thoughts, feelings, and intent. Then a listener must decode this message through a filter of their own biases, attitudes, beliefs, feelings, motives, and life experiences. And to make it more complex, experts in a rule of 7-38-55,[12] tell us that words make up only about 7% of the message in face-to-face communication.[4] The tone of voice is about 38% of the message and body language, as well as

---

[12] 7-38-55 rule: 38% tone of voice, 55% body language. Mehrabian, A., & Wiener, M. (1967). Mehrabian, A., & Wiener, M. (1967). Decoding of inconsistent communications. Journal of Personality and Social Psychology, 6, 109–114.pdf, 6(1), 109–114.

other contextual cues, make up about 55%. Although exact percentages are hard to come by, it is true that there is simply a lot going on which can make deep listening challenging. That is why a message in an email only communicates about 7% of the entire message and text messages communicate less than 2%. I have often suggested that we get together in person when someone wants to convey more than just information.

A Definition of Deep Listening

Deep listening is suspending judgment and being fully present with another person to understand the experience or point of view. Deep listening involves hearing more than the words of the speaker but taps into the deeper meaning, unspoken needs, and feelings conveyed. It is something that is done with the *heart* as well as the mind.

So, deep listening begins with accurately perceiving what others are saying. The message sent will equal the message received. If simply transmitting information, such as the time or place of a meeting, an email or text message is enough. All other communication needs thoughtful, deep, attention and consideration.

Again, in conversation, there is much more than facts being conveyed. To listen well, we have to understand that people want and need to be heard. They want to know that their opinions matter. They want empathy and respect. Empathy is doing our best to experience the world and situation from their point of view. Respect is offering due regard for their opinions, feelings, needs, and personhood. This is a necessary ingredient of the church of the future. It is also a necessary ingredient to a feeling of inclusion in our communities today.

It is by deep listening that we grant these gifts of empathy and respect. Listening shows that we not only understand what they are saying but that we value and respect them as human beings. Through deep listening we not only communicate information but affirm and support others as well as build and transform relationships. This is a primary and key objective in any spiritually centered relationship.

There are a lot of benefits that come from deep listening. Through deep listening we:

- Gain rapport with others.
- Build trust and goodwill.
- Deepen our understanding of others.
- Learn innovative ideas and perspectives.
- Make it safe for others to open so we're dealing with deep and not surface issues.
- Gain accurate information for better decision-making and problem-solving.
- Overcome friction and work through conflict.
- Develop shared understanding and consensus.
- Affirm, motivate, and empower others.
- Promote personal and relationship healing.

Good deep listening is at the very heart of *all* healthy relationships, including the work we do in spiritual communities. Good listening matters. It matters in our relationship with friends, spouses, or partners. Listening matters in our relationship with our children and grandchildren. It matters to those who collaborate with us as well as our customers, our peers, and our co-workers. It matters to the people around us. It matters to those that visit our churches and evaluate if they want to stay.

Our ability to improve our deep listening skills can improve or even transform each of these relationships. People will notice that we are present and attuned. They will be drawn to our influence and leadership. As we learn and practice this skill, we'll build better relationships, achieve better results and have more satisfying and successful relationships. Period.

And yet we are not good listeners. We listen to respond rather than to understand. Our minds think at about

400 words per minute and yet we speak only 125 words per minute which means we get distracted and fail to give others our full attention. We are quick to judge what they're saying and agree or disagree, think we already know, or we give advice, fix problems, dismiss, or one-up other people rather than hear what they are really saying.

Unfortunately, most of us are not good listeners. We tend to be involved in:

• Distracting - Getting distracted by random thoughts or what's something else going on.

• Interpretating - Interpret what others say through filters (biases, feelings, motives, experiences)

• Tuning Out - Tuning out because we already know what someone is going to say.

• Judging Importance - Thinking that what others have to say isn't important.

• Planning Response - Focusing on formulating our own response.

• Judging - Quickly judging (agreeing or disagreeing) rather than opening ourselves to another point of view.

• Impatience - Impatient for someone to finish so we can talk.

• Shutting Down - Shut down messages we don't want to hear.

• Deeper Meaning – Considering the words only and not the deeper needs or meaning.

• Taking Over - Take over the conversation by comments and questions.

• Offer solutions - Suggest "quick fixes" rather than guiding others to their own wisdom and experience.

• Fix - Trying to make others feel better rather than letting others own and work through their experience.

In our spiritual centers it is no different. Over the years I have attended hundreds of staff and board meetings. The norm is to go from conversation to conversation, often changing subjects, fixing opinions, declaring an idea will not work or is unimportant, interrupting, and being centered in planning the next contribution while another is speaking. Seldom is there space to digest and consider what has just been said.

And the same can be said about the conversations with those that visit our communities. We often cut conversations short because we are obligated to greet visitors, but we really want to connect with our own friends and loved ones.

Even when heartfelt needs are expressed, we often want to fix the attitude or offer some metaphysical advice instead of our hearts. An example is this elderly widower in assisted living:

He recently broke his leg from a fall and was told he would need surgery and then he would go to a nursing home for rehabilitation.

Hearing this was very traumatic to this man. His immediate reaction was, "I don't want surgery. Can't it heal on its own? If they take me to a nursing home, I'll never make it back to assisted living." His caregivers reassured him that he'd be okay. "Don't worry about this...." "Don't worry about that...." "You are going to be fine." These were loving responses. However, they failed to respond to his deeper feelings and fears.

I would suggest that this person needs someone to just listen. "It had to be so hard to learn that you'd broken your leg." "Having a surgery is very frightening." "It would be so hard if you couldn't come back here." Then listen…and listen…and let him talk.

Once he's talked and been heard, he'll be more open to influence and input. "This is why the surgery is important." "You may have to go to a nursing home, but the goal is to bring you back to assisted living." "This is a tough thing you're going through. How would you like to face it?"

Rachel Naomi Remen, M.D. shared an idea that pertains to spiritual communities in *Kitchen Table Wisdom*.[13] She writes:

"I suspect that the most basic and powerful way to connect to another person is to listen. Just listen. Perhaps the most important thing we ever give each other is our attention. And especially if it's given from the heart. When people are talking, there's no need to do anything but receive them. Just take them in. Listen to what they are saying. Care about it. Most times caring about it is even more important than understanding it. Most of us don't value ourselves or love ourselves enough to know this. It has taken me a long time to believe in the power of simply saying, "I'm so sorry," when someone is in pain. And meaning it.

"One of my patients told me that when she tried to tell her story people often interrupted to tell her that they once had something just like that happen to them. Subtly her pain became a story about themselves. Eventually she stopped talking to most people. It was just too lonely.

"I have even learned to respond to someone crying by just listening. In the old days I used to reach for the tissues, until I realized that passing a person a tissue may be just another way to shut them down, to take them out of their experience of sadness and grief. Now I just listen. When they have cried all, they need to cry, they find me there with them."

"This simple thing has not been that easy to learn. I thought people listened only because they were too timid to speak or did not know the answer. A loving silence often has

---

[13] Remen, Rachel. *Kitchen Table Wisdom: Stories that Heal*, Riverhead Books, 2006

far more power to heal and to connect than the most well-intentioned words."

A Parting Thought about Deep Listening

We often think that the most important influencing skill is being able to explain ourselves more eloquently or forcefully. It is important to present our Unity principles and have interesting and informative services and programs in our churches. However, I have had many explain that the relationships they value most and what draws them to Unity are those relationships in which someone has listened and really heard them. These relationships have not only helped them feel validated and affirmed but have given them the desire and courage to improve or go forward to accomplish important things. A caring heart has done more to attract others than all the inspirational messages that we can present.

Perhaps it is through our presence and willingness to listen deeply, rather than offering our advice, that we offer others one of the most precious gifts of all, deep listening. It is that gift that will further the impact of our spiritual centers into the future.

Chapter 6 - Suspension of Certainty

Transcendent discovery is far more possible for individuals and "If your mind is groups when there is a willingness to empty, it is always risk, to admit, or to not know. The ready for anything, it capacity to create together depends on is open to everything. the suspension of any one individual or In the beginner's subgroup always being in the right. This mind there are many commitment to suspend certainty is possibilities, but in what makes our knowing together the expert's mind collective, because something new and there are few unexpected things that often emerge in and through the group. A greater collective wisdom becomes possible because ideas are no longer the possession of one person but are shared by those that helped shape it together. A suspension of certainty is akin to a beginner's mind, a commitment to not know so that new knowledge can arise.

It is not just something we practice when we're learning something — though dropping the "expert's mind" and seeing the learning as a beginner is an important practice in learning. It's something we can practice every single moment of the day.

What is beginner's mind? It's dropping our expectations and preconceived ideas about anything, and seeing things with an open mind, fresh eyes, just like a beginner. If you've ever learned something new, you can remember what that's like: you're probably confused, because you don't know how to do whatever you're learning, but you're also looking at everything as if it's brand new, perhaps with curiosity and wonder. That is beginner's mind.

Why It Matters

When we practice beginner's mind with in making decisions:

- Better experiences: We aren't clouded by prejudgments, preconceptions, fantasies about what it should be or assumptions about how we already know it will be. When we don't have these, we can't be disappointed or frustrated by the experience, because there's no fantasy or preconception to compare it to.
- Better relationships: If we are talking to someone, instead of being frustrated because they aren't meeting our time or other expectations, we can see them with fresh eyes and notice that they're just trying to be happy, that they have good intentions (even if they're not your intentions), and they are struggling just like all of us. This transforms our relationship with the person.
- Less procrastination: If we are procrastinating on a big task, we can look at it with beginner's mind and instead of worrying about how hard the task will be or how we might fail at it … we can be curious about what the task will be like. We can notice the details of doing the task, instead of trying to get away from them.
- Less anxiety: If we have an upcoming event or meeting that we're anxious about … instead of worrying about what might happen, we can open ourselves to being curious about what will happen, let go of our preconceived ideas about the outcome and embrace not knowing, embrace being present and finding gratitude in the moment for what we're doing and who we're doing it with.

As you can see, the practice of beginner's mind can transform any activity, minimizes difficulties, allows more flexibility, and enhances openness, curiosity, gratefulness, and allows being present. This will attract collective wisdom to us.

How to Practice

Beginner's mind can be practiced in meditation. Instead of sitting in meditation and thinking we know what our breath will be like, or the present moment will be like … pay attention. See it with fresh eyes. Drop preconceived ideas and just look clearly at what is there.

Daily meditation practice is extremely useful in developing this beginner's mind. Here is how to practice:

1. Sit comfortably and upright in a quiet place.

2. Pay attention to your body, then your breath, trying to see them clearly and freshly.

3. When you notice yourself having preconceived ideas, wandering from the present moment, thinking you know how it will be … just notice that.

4. See if you can drop the ideas and thoughts and fantasies and stories that are filling up your head. Empty yourself so you can see what's in front of you. See what your breath is actually like, right now, instead of what you think it will be or what you're thinking about.

Repeat the last few steps, over and over. See the thoughts and fantasies, empty yourself and see what's there with fresh eyes.

You can practice this right now, with whatever is in front of you. With how your body feels, how your breath feels, whatever else is around you.

You can practice whenever you do any activity, from brushing your teeth to washing the dishes to walking and driving and working out and using your phone.

You can practice whenever you talk to another human being, dropping your ideas of how they should be or ought to be. Empty your mind and see them as they truly are. Notice their good heart, see their difficulties with compassion, and be grateful for them as they are. Love them for who they are and find compassion for their struggles.

[41]

Practice it when you are in a meeting. Be curious about what will arise. Remove all preconceived ideas, fears, and expectations from your mind. Go to your heart space and listen with compassion.

This is the practice. Do it with love, with fresh eyes and gratitude for the only situation we'll ever get — the actual one in front of us. This is the second principle in drawing collective wisdom to us. This principle should be clear in that it is obvious we cannot draw to us fresh insight if we enter situations with preconceived notions that it won't work, it will fail, or we have tried it before! This is another best practice that will lead to decisions based upon collective wisdom.

Chapter 7 – Seek Diverse Perspectives

You've probably heard it before — seek input, be inclusive, welcome perspectives, collaborate with others. But why? Where does this premise come from and why is this type of inclusion beneficial for individuals, teams, or organizations?

In a recent meeting, we discussed the effectiveness of different learning strategies. The topic got us thinking about the similarities and differences that exist from person to person, learning or otherwise. We briefly discussed strength finders, Myers-Briggs Type Inventory, and other tests that help people understand themselves and others better.

Although I believe these assessments are merely tools of understanding and not a diagnosis, it made me think about the diversity of thought and how our individual traits tie into the bigger picture of a church.

Imagine, for example, church leadership made up of only ESTJ personality types (extroverted, sensing, thinking, and judging). An organization like this would be missing out on the valuable perspectives of introverts, intuitives, feelers, and perceivers, and any other combination of the eight different traits. This would inevitably limit our church by limiting our ability to provide a something worthwhile and meaningful that has been approached and devised from "all angles." Decisions and our overall ministry are limited when perspectives are limited.

The Fierce Team Model[14] uses the term "beach ball" to describe how perspectives occur within churches. Each person, from every level within the organization, has their own color stripe on the beach ball. Of course, it takes all the

---

[14] https://fierceinc.com/the-fierce-approach-to-team-management/ [7] https://www.scientificamerican.com/article/how-diversity-makes-ussmarter/

individual stripes coming together collectively to make up the beach ball.

The beach ball analogy comes from the idea that no single person holds the whole truth, but rather a mere sliver or "stripe" of it. And every stripe counts.

An article from *Scientific American* titled "How Diversity Makes Us Smarter"[7] states that "decades of research by organizational scientists, psychologists, sociologists, economists, and demographers show that socially diverse groups (that is, those with a diversity of race, ethnicity, gender, and sexual orientation) are more innovative than homogeneous groups."

Although the focus should be geared toward diversity of thought regardless of a social group, this finding illustrates that when individuals from different walks of life come together and share unique viewpoints, positive results increase.

Without diversity of thought, innovation is thwarted, initiatives may stall, and you alone cannot save your church. You need to approach issues with several perspectives to be able to see the whole truth.

Barriers to Creating More Inclusion

While seeking input sounds easy enough, many organizations struggle to follow through. Here are some of the barriers that often arise.

We're afraid our own perspective won't be good enough. Our perspective is valid, and it matters, but it is limited by our own experience. There's no way around this fact, and it's true for everyone. Our egos would like us to believe that we have all the answers, or that our way is the best way, and we want to be perceived by others as competent. But there are other people to consider, including the people who we will impact. It's bigger than just us.

What we must accept is that someone else in the room may have a better idea, and that's ok.

We invite the wrong people to the table.

What occurs too often is that leaders will invite a select few to the critical conversations, and these "favorites" may not be the only people you need to speak with. Consider who the decision will impact and set hierarchies aside — seek input from various levels, and actively take these alternative perspectives into account when finalizing a decision.

Deep cultural problems have yet to be addressed.

Perhaps in your church, being inclusive isn't the norm. Would it be unusual to host a meeting where the intention is to share perspectives? Are there silos between teams and departments? Do leaders fail to give and ask for feedback? If so, you could be facing some deep cultural issues that need some serious adjustment.

The most effective, long-term solution is leadership training, and we can get started today in shifting our church's current mindset by seeking input from someone on a current decision we're facing, especially someone we may not typically involve in the process. Explain the situation fully and ask them what they think about it.

The rewards of overcoming the barriers and creating more inclusion are worth it.

If we want to form an inclusive environment where other perspectives are welcomed, the focus should be on getting curious and expanding our thinking.

Here are some actions to overcome barriers and ignite a more inclusive culture:

1.   Host a Beach Ball meeting.

Even if we've never participated in the Fierce Team Program, we can still apply the concept of the model. Start by identifying an issue in need of resolution and invite key influencers to the meeting. Before the meeting, provide them with the issue at hand, why it matters, the ideal outcome, and what help we would like.

When we need to decide or move a project forward, multiple heads are always better than one. I can't tell how many times I've sat in a meeting and thought holy cow, I never thought of that! And the action steps we take following one of these meetings are always more informed and beneficial for the church.

2.   Abandon "right and wrong."

Sure, there are times when objectivity is needed, and data doesn't lie. But when it comes to our approach toward the perspectives of others, especially when subjectivity plays a role, it's important to be open by avoiding the labels of "right" or "wrong" when we invite others' ideas to the table. Instead, reframe right and wrong to what "will work" or "won't work" for the matter at hand.

Consider the following question:

Based on all the perspectives that have been shared, what's ultimately the best decision for the church?

3.   Practice inclusion without illusion.

Don't just implement inclusion initiatives for the sake of best practices. Do so out of genuine curiosity and interest. We need to check in with ourselves regarding our approach—if we don't believe another's input to be valid or worth hearing, chances are, they will be able to pick up on it and see that we're brushing their perspective under the rug. We need to remind ourselves that every stripe has value (regardless of organizational level) and listen with an open mind.

An added benefit to inviting diverse perspectives is that on an individual level, we feel appreciated and heard. Knowing that our own stripe is being considered, regardless of the outcome, is a good feeling.

Leaders need to leverage the strengths that vary from person to person as well as our unique contexts, preferences, and life experiences. And contributors, bring all of who we are to the conversation because every unique experience of the world is valid. Every perspective matters. We're all moving in the direction toward a common goal in our church, and when everyone contributes their perspective to this goal, we can get there more efficiently, more effectively, and more successfully.

Do you want to attract a diverse congregation? Is your congregation made up of individuals that are pretty much the same? If that is so and you wish it to be different, look at who is on the Sunday platform and who is in leadership.

Chapter 8 – Group Discernment

This process assumes that all involved share the characteristics vital for discernment: a desire to discern, self-knowledge, humility, courage, a commitment deep listening, and the seeking of diverse opinions. In addition, group discernment rests on the conviction that collective wisdom comes most fully through a group and depends on members' willingness to trust the wisdom of the group.

Group discernment cannot work if we come to decision-making groups with our own agendas, ready to lobby for our own ideas and advocate for our own values. If we bring this fixed attitude, we will simply argue on behalf of our own agendas and try to persuade others to join our side. Group discernment looks not for a majority vote but for clarity about what collective wisdom desires us to be and do.

Self-centered attitudes destroy group discernment. Members of the group must come with only one agenda: to listen for the collective wisdom of the group. Instead of believing that he or she has the complete answer, each member comes to the group trusting that he or she brings some tiny piece of wisdom that will be valuable in the process. Only by putting all the group's pieces of wisdom together will true wisdom emerge, a whole greater than the sum of its parts. Each member looks for the direction and waits for a sense of heartfelt unanimity.

Group discernment is meant to work primarily in small groups or teams, not in the larger congregational meeting. It is meant to be exercised in board or team discussions. Each member of the group shares their wisdom and inclination. Each member practices deep listening. Silence and questions, not challenges, are part of the process. Then the group compares insights and works toward unanimity. Each member of the group is asked if they can agree with or live with the group consensus. If not, the group continues to explore differences until the small group reaches that point of agreement.

At Unity of Sun City, the Board of Trustees always worked and attained consensus as it practiced group discernment. Although meetings were open, members of the congregation seldom attended. Why? Although financial and progress reports were discussed, the meetings were about checking in on Board members, and discussions by Board Members about current issues. There were few decisions for change. Change decisions were made by staff members or team members in the congregation. The real action was in the congregational teams. Board meetings were about deep listening, group discernment and reporting (celebrating) on all that was arising.

Chapter 9 - Welcome All that is Arising.

Mindfulness-based cognitive therapy takes a mindfully accepting attitude towards *all* experiences by suggesting the importance of "laying out the red carpet" for unwanted or diverse experiences or situations. Invite them in or else they will stay for a *long* time. Resist them and they will persist. Imagine that you have just had an argument and you are experiencing a range of distressing feelings: anxiety/fear, anger, or sadness. Maybe you're even feeling a bit guilty for something that you have said or done.

In this situation, it is understandable to have a deep desire to *not* feel these feelings. Some people react to unwanted thoughts or feelings by pretending they don't exist. They minimize their importance or avoid the person/situation who activates the negative feelings.

When we try to *avoid* thoughts and feelings, they really *don't* go away? There must be a better solution than denial and avoidance.

There is a solution – *welcoming* what is. When we fully welcome and accept *all* thoughts and feelings, we are no longer caught in a *struggle* with them… we are no longer *fighting* what is. Remind yourself that in no way does acceptance mean approval any more than it means resignation or giving up. In fact, all that you are "giving up" is the choice to continue to struggle and suffer over a preference or an opinion.

It is somewhat paradoxical that when we truly open ourselves to accept where we are, *then* we are open to change and growth. Through mindfulness practices, it is possible to learn how to welcome "what is" in the constantly unfolding present moment. In fact, we can even take things a step further by expressing *gratitude* for diverse situations.

If you have a tendency to push down, minimize, or deny thoughts and feelings, try meeting your next uncomfortable internal experience with a different attitude and *see what*

[51]

happens. Imagine that you are still feeling those lingering feelings of anger, sadness, or fear resulting from an argument. Rather than avoid those feelings at all costs, try something different: "I notice myself feeling anger/sadness/fear." "I fully accept these feelings." "These feelings are temporary."

Mindfulness-Based Cognitive Therapy[15] is a practice that points out the underpinning learning that supports acceptance:

•   Be aware of sensations in your body to anchor you to the present moment.

•   Practice *responding* to these sensations from a connected place with others, rather than *reacting* from a disconnected place.

•   Move from "avoidance mode" to "approach mode" by cultivating an open and curious attitude towards *all* experiences and opinions.

•   See with absolute clarity the unnecessary suffering that avoidance causes.

•   Choose an attitude of *allowing*, rather than forcing things to be different than they are.

Life inevitably brings a feeling of sadness because of the illusion of loss. Change brings a sense of loss for all that was familiar and maybe even self-created. The important thing to recognize is that *suffering* is optional. If we are truly ready to break free from emotional suffering, mindfulness-based approaches to treatment have valuable tools that we can learn about and practice in our life. It all starts with our attitude and the choices that we make.

Today, truly *welcome* "what is."

Welcoming what is instead of what used to be is important as we move into the future of spiritual centers. Society is moving away from religions as they used to be.

---

[15] Crane, R. *Mindfulness-based cognitive therapy.* New York, NY: Routledge, 2009

There are changes taking place in our post-pandemic world. A new reality will emerge, and it will be different than we think. It will disappoint those of us that love the church of our childhood or even the church we experienced even a decade ago.

Every church and every leader has a model of their imaginary church. Even those who claim they don't have a model, have a model. Their anti-model is the model. A model is simply an approach—a strategy, a way of doing things. The old model of Church has been proving less effective year by year for decades across almost all denominations and traditions. Unfortunately, we must remind ourselves of the situations causing change in spiritual centers of all types. We must recognize that these changes have or will happen even as we wish it is not so.

In 2021, Gallup shared that for the first time ever, church membership dropped below 50% nationally.

Among Millennials, only 36% identify with a church. Similarly, a decade ago only 22% of Millennials said they have no religious affiliation. Today that number is 31%. For Gen Z, 33% now say they have no religious affiliation.[16]

At the same time, attendance keeps dropping across the board. A survey by FACT of over 15,000 churches conducted just before COVID hit shows that between 2000 and 2020, median church service attendance of all churches dropped from 137 people to 65. A median attendance at Unity and CSL churches is less than 40.

---

[16] The latest 2024 poll: Three in 10 Americans say they attend religious services every week (21%) or almost every week (9%), while 11% report attending about once a month and 56% seldom (25%) or never (31%) attend.

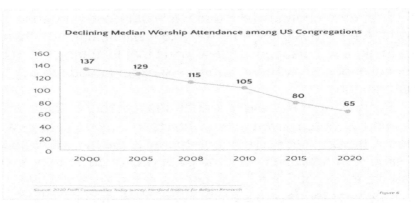

Declining Median Worship Attendance among US Congregations

Source: 2020 Faith Communities Today Survey, Hartford Institute for Religion Research   Figure 6

2022 should start to yield data on where things stand now, and as you already suspect, the new data is highly likely to show further decline. In other words, even if your church returns to 2019 attendance levels or exceeds them, the overall decline in church attendance will continue unabated.

So, what does this mean?

The *current* approach to church not only isn't effective, but it also hasn't been effective for decades. Yet leaders keep moving forward as though somehow things are going to turn around. Optimism is one thing. Delusion is another.

The death of an approach to church doesn't equal the death of the Church. There are still millions that have an interest in and are inspired by spirituality. Changing the approach is the best way to begin to see new growth. Wise leaders will become students of what's happening and seek to find a new approach that's culturally effective. As Mark Sayers pointed out in his Rebuilders Podcast, the model of church is actually being rebuilt right now…as we speak. Maybe leaders, such as ministers and pastors aren't doing it, but *people* are doing it. They are those in your pews that are interested and engaged even as we may not be giving them the permission to lead into new ways of doing church. Rightly or wrongly, they're deciding how and when to engage with church, and they're voting with their feet and wallets.

Adept leaders will figure out where culture is going, figure out how to meet people where they're at, and then lead them to where they want to be. What was is gone. What will be hasn't yet emerged. Some of the ideas expressed by church visionaries include:

1. The key is to experiment. Be more inclusive. Be more broad in the subjects of Sunday lessons and classes. Include others in presenting talks and music. There are those in your pews with a lifetime of experience and spiritual growth.

2. Innovate beyond weekend services. With youth sports dominating Sunday mornings maybe a Fun Friday Night for families may attract more youth. 3. Form a vision for the future that is clearly stated. Find a new approach that's resonating and begin to reach new people. Maybe a neighborhood children's event may attract your neighbors.

4. Hybrid church will simply become the way church is. But you will have to invest in technology to make it something that is needed and wanted.

5. Information or Unity principles will move online, and application will move to in-person events at unexpected times and places.

6. Location-independent church members will increase. You will be including individuals from diverse places, including internationally.

7. Ministers and spiritual leaders will sense diminished authority. Minister-centric churches will be less effective and less desirable to potential congregants. We, that is, us clergy, will develop into coaches, encouragers, and resource individuals.

8.

Chapter 10 - Trust in Transcendent Wisdom

We have the desire to catch hold of the One and capture it within the walls of a temple, a mosque, or a church, where we have been taught to believe the One resides. We call its God's house. We cannot name the One who resides there, although we try. We may call it God or Goddess, Allah, Christ, or Lord. We discover that the One cannot rightly be called He, although tradition required that we assign a pronoun to the Formless. We cannot define the One as we define a tree, a bird, or a friend, although we try.

We claim the One for our tribe alone, but then we see it everywhere; in an airport where a man unrolls a small rug and bends to press his forehead to the ground in submission; in the storefront church of the inner city where poor people sing and weep at the same time; in the great cathedral where a grandmother, her head covered, knells before the altar where the form of another woman rests and is known as the very Mother of God. We soon recognize our God as everyone's God.

And not only among Jews, and Christians and Muslims do we see the reflection of the face of the One. When the land ends and we gaze out on a thousand miles of water, there is the One. When the mother pushes through pain and the infant takes in its first breath, there is the One. When the father in a military cemetery drops to his knees after burying his only son, there is the One. In our first kiss and our final embrace, there is the One.

The One shows up in native lodges and Hindu temples, in the deep quiet of Zen meditation halls and in the ecstatic whirling of Sufi dervishes. The One whispers through the words of ancient poets, through the creative art of the painters, sculptors, and woodcarvers; through symphony and rap rhythm; Gregorian chants, hymns of praise, devotional songs. Also, through tobacco and cornmeal offered at dawn to the Great Spirit.

The One makes its appearance in the heart of the self-described atheist, who gasps in awe at the newly fallen snows, carpeting the garden with jewels of frozen light.

The One reveals itself as the compassionate father and the protective mother as well as the loyal friend. It resides always at the core of our hearts; utterly invisible. The One transcends all form, all descriptions, all theory, refusing to be defined or contained. It resists our human impulse to unlock the mystery or imagine it as a person with qualities, thoughts, and personality like our own. The One resides at the center of all that is, ever-present and totally available.

It is the still, small voice that speaks when we enter the silence. It is love, wisdom, understanding, and all knowledge. It gives everything and requires nothing.

We remember, we forget, and we remember again. It is called by a thousand names, limited by none. It is you; it is me. It is everything.

The writer of Proverbs summed up the need to reach the wisdom of the One:

"Sell everything and buy Wisdom! Forage for Understanding! Don't forget one word! Don't deviate an inch! Never walk away from Wisdom—she guards your life; love her—she keeps her eye on you. Above all and before all, do this: Get Wisdom!

Write this at the top of your list: Get Understanding! Throw your arms around her—believe me, you won't regret it; never let her go—she'll make your life glorious. She'll garland your life with grace, she'll festoon your days with beauty."

Trust in Wisdom

The greatest spiritual teachers of all ages have encouraged us to seek wisdom. How do we seek wisdom? Wisdom is more than knowledge; it is sound judgment and discernment. It is knowing what to pursue and what to let go, what to long for and what to flee. Where does wisdom come from? "The fear of the Lord is the beginning of wisdom; all who follow his precepts have good understanding."[17] "If any of you lacks wisdom, you should ask God, who gives generously to all without finding fault, and it will be given to you."[18]

Here are six gems of wisdom which a friend of Norman Vincent Peale repeats almost every day:

1.   "To live long, live slowly."—Cicero
2.   "The way of a superior man is threefold: virtuous, he is therefore free from anxiety; wise, he is therefore free from perplexity; bold, he is therefore free from fear."— Confucius
3.   "Sit loosely in the saddle of life."—Robert Louis Stevenson
"Let nothing disturb you; let nothing frighten you. Everything passes except God; God alone is sufficient."— Saint Theresa
4.   "In quietness and in confidence shall be your strength."—Isaiah 30:15
5.   Then finally, and most importantly, the words of Jesus: "Peace I leave with you; my peace I give you. I do not give to you as the world gives. Do not let your hearts be troubled and do not be afraid" (John 14:27).

---

[17] Psalm 111:10
[18] James 1:5

Wisdom, like the One, is always present and is accessible at any moment.

A human being is Divinity in expression. We call this the Christ Presence within us. Our very essence is God, and therefore humans are inherently good. Our relationship with God is paradoxical — God is our essence, *and* we are not fully aware of it. Our continuous spiritual awakening and development is necessary to mature our ability to live our Christ identity.

So, to restate postulates or axioms that are generally agreed to by the mystical expressions of world religions to form a base understanding, we might agree with many of these statements:

.

• We are the expression of the Divine, always have been, always will be since the beginning of time.

• The connection is so deep and true that we can never be separated from that Source.

• We can ignore it or suppress it, but it is always there, beckoning us to open our heart and partake of Divine wisdom.

• The voice in our heart is that of the Divine Source guiding our life.

• We are not to ignore those whispers speaking to us. There is universal truth, guiding us with unfathomable wisdom.

• We are to remember our Divine origins and touch that Divine Source within. We are to accept the Divine hand guiding all of life. We are to acknowledge this deep truth and wisdom in us and rise in our power.

• Those qualities are everywhere present and universally present in all life.

Chapter 11 – Questions for Discussion

Our attempt has been to give the basic thoughts and ideas about spiritual centers and how the church of the future must depend on collective wisdom to overcome the post-pandemic forces, ideas, and traditions that continue to make them irrelevant in the 21st century. The church of tomorrow will be different than the church of yesterday.

Rather than give direct recommendations and solutions to all types of spiritual organizations, we give foundations. The specifics will arise out of collective wisdom. We do know, however, that collective wisdom only arises out of certain conditions: deep listening, suspension of certainty, the inclusion of diverse perspectives; an attitude of welcoming all that is arising; and a deep trust in transcendent wisdom that is always present and always at work.

So, perhaps questions for your discussion is the best approach to summarizing what has been said:

1.   What does the church of the future look like for you? How will it include what has been valuable in the past? How will it be different?

a.   What will be the role of the spiritual leader?[19]

b.   What will be the role of the Board or Council?[20]

c.   What will be the expectations of the Millennials and future generations?

2.   Why is collective wisdom important? To what extent is collective wisdom at work in your church? Is it wisdom, opinion, or preferences?

---

[19] See Appendix I

[20] See Appendix II

3.　　　To what extent do we practice deep listening in our boards, teams, staff meetings, with visitors, with members? What are our plans to practice this skill? Do we need a class or discussion group on the subject?

4.　　　As ideas are presented, is there deep listening, dismissal, an embrace of certainty or tradition in the outcome? How can we work from a "beginner's mind"?

5.　　　How can we seek diverse opinions? Diversity includes ages, involvement, personality traits and a host of other factors.

6.　　　How do we practice group discernment? Do all individuals have an equal voice? Do we practice discernment and work through disagreement?

7.　　　How do we welcome all that has and is arising? This includes difficulties, lack of resources, disagreements.

8.　　　What is our view of the influence of the transcendent at work in our midst?

In chapter 2, we will tell you a little about what we have done to further collective wisdom at Unity of Fort Collins, Colorado.

Chapter 12 – Implementation

Implementation of a team-based management and governance initiative in a spiritual center when there are other problems in relationships between Spiritual Leaders, the Board, and members is probably questionable. The relationship deficits will still exist; teams do not solve deep-seated conflict.

If the ministry is otherwise healthy, the implementation will succeed if it is approached wisely, prayerfully and in consensus with all leaders of the ministry, both formal and informal. Here are some considerations and suggestions for implementation.

1.   Is the Spiritual Leader on board? The Spiritual Leader sample agreement in Appendix I needs to be reviewed. Is the Spiritual Leader willing to be a facilitator, coach and encourager rather than centric to the programs of the ministry? Is that leader willing to take a back seat even when that leader, due to training or experience, may be able to be more qualified?

2.   Are the elected board members on board, by consensus? Are they willing to release day-to-day operations to teams and major on issues of vision and governance. A careful review of material in Appendix II is needed.

3.   Who are the other formal or informal leaders? Office managers, licensed Unity teachers, long-term members, contributors, patriarchs and matriarchs? You may want to hold small discussion meetings where the ideas are shared, questioned, and discussed.

4.   Set a road map of where you want to begin and where you want to end... some months or years in the future. It doesn't have to be a program that upsets all existing culture and programs. Some parts of the ministry may be working well and there is no need to fix what works.

5.		Work with a portion of the ministry. There may already be teams of individuals that work well together. There may be a finance team, a social team (we call it connections) that can be used as examples of team successes.

6.		Form one or two new teams as small groups that meet immediate needs of the ministry. Examples may be a welcoming team or a marketing team. Hold a discussion about team leadership principles, gain some new volunteers, coach the team, assign a budget if required and turn them loose on their inspired creativity.

7.		Remember that the end game or purpose is not to get free labor. It is to form a team as a small group and incorporate individuals in ownership of an important part of the ministry; ownership, inclusion, and engagement.

8.		Open other ministry opportunities to parts of the community such as readings, speaking... Yes, many individuals can and will present interesting and life-changing challenges in sharing their spiritual journeys.

Work in small ways in those areas that will build success and, therefore successful stories will be told and examples will be shared. To some, these ideas are radically different. We are building a community based spiritual and team-centered principles. We could stick with what is not working and has not worked. That may be easier, but in doing so we will be the church of the past instead of the community of the future.

Appendix I – Sample Spiritual Leader Agreement

Duties and Reporting Relationship. As the Spiritual Leaders, you are part of the Support team and the Council and also report to the Council.

Salary. Your salary will be an monthly rate of $000, paid as manse expense on the final day of each month.

Other Reimbursement. Unity of Fort Collins will reimburse you for any otherwise unreimbursed Unity Convention, Unity Worldwide Ministry service, and other Council approved workshop expenses. This includes travel and lodging. This is subject to the budget allocation of the Finance Team and the Council.

Unity of Fort Collins will reimburse you for necessary office, book, class or other expenses subject to the budget allocation of the Finance Team and the Council

Benefits and Time Off. Unity of Fort Collins currently offers no benefits such as health insurance coverage, and as a 501(c)3 organization, UFC is exempt from paying federal and state unemployment taxes. As a salaried employee, you may take reasonable holidays, vacation, and personal time off. This is subject to the approval of the Council. This approval is contingent upon all responsibilities listed below being covered.

Ethics. As a condition of your employment, you were required to sign and continue to comply with the Unity Worldwide Ministries Ethics Agreement. Your employment with UFC is contingent upon continued satisfactory results of a background check periodically performed pursuant to your written authorization.

At-Will Employment Relationship. Your employment is not for any fixed period, and it is terminable at-will. Thus, either you or UFC may terminate your employment relationship at any time, with or without cause, and with or without advance notice. Although not required, UFC requests that you provide at least one month advance written notice of your resignation, to permit you and UFC to arrange for a smooth transition of the ministry and attend to other matters relating to your departure.

Responsibilities. Your responsibilities include and your performance is evaluated based on these duties that have been mutually agreed upon:

- As a Spiritual Leader, you are primarily an encourager, coach, and resource individual for the Council, the ministry teams, and for individuals.
- You work collaboratively with the Council, staff, music leader in the format and content of all church services, classes and other activities. Also collaborate on general spiritual direction of the ministry.
- Work collaboratively with teams, not as a supervisor, but as a coach and resource person. Teams are assigned to co-ministers based on need and interest. Examples:
- Sharon: Chaplain, Facilities, Finance (Accounting), Support (Music), YFM
- Jim: Connection, Facilities, Finance (Fundraising), Outreach, Support (Services), Technology, Welcome
- As requested, officiate at Sunday services and special services, such as weddings and memorials.
- As requested, provide pastoral counseling
- Conduct classes and approve classes in accordance with Unity philosophy and teachings
- Assist with selection of books offered in the bookstore

- Contribute articles for printed newsletter, newsletter and other publicity pieces in cooperation with the Marketing team.
- Review finances/Budget with the Treasurer and/or Finance Team prior to Council meetings, so there is a deep understanding of finances.
- Represent Unity of Fort Collins in the community at large by participating in Community Business Organization and Ecumenical organizations, events, and meetings
- Work cooperatively with the Council and teams to sponsor events and fundraising activities that reflect and promote Unity of Fort Collins in the surrounding community.

Appendix II – Rethinking Boards

Bill Habict is a blogger at Pedestrian People. His recent blog was entitled, *Why Church Boards Need to Die.*

Why does he say that? He gives five reasons. Without much explanation, I am sure you can agree with some of them.

1.   Church Boards generally serve in a management capacity. While visioning is part of their duties, there's simply too much on their plates to allow for creative, long-term, outside the-box visioning.

2.   Church Boards are largely comprised of Shepherds, not Entrepreneurs. They generally want to deepen the group, care for the flock, not innovate. These are all good things, but the church today is flooded with leaders who fit the Shepherd model, caring for people already assembled, managing what's been built and helping meet people's needs.

3.   Church Boards are largely comprised of folks who like the church as it is. Nothing else needs to be said about this.

4.   Church Boards are homogeneous. Beyond, the "you need to be a church member" and "you need to take certain classes" there's often other requirements that undermine diversity. Including is one of the requirements for collective wisdom and it is seldom found on a Church Board.

5.   Church Boards seldom embrace any of the other components of collective wisdom. Embracing what arises, deep listening, or any of the others.

So, what do Church Boards do? We know that churches rely on the donations of members to fund a mission. Members enjoy a tax deduction for these donations that are freely given to churches that maintain nonprofit status with the IRS. One of the requirements for maintaining a nonprofit status is to have an oversight board. Council responsibilities are many but the most important is to ensure that the ministry is financially viable and that it fulfills its core mission. This is done by developing strategy, monitoring performance and ensuring church financial accountability for the sacrificed donations. The council makes certain a meaningful mission is implemented effectively.

Effective councils have an impact on the long-term viability of the organization and have a vested interest in how well the church implements the strategy of achieving its mission. This is done by meeting regularly while actively overseeing the key operational functions – which are church budget oversight, top leader performance evaluation, strategic performance management, and legal compliance.

1. Strategic Planning

The council is responsible for articulating the church's core mission and developing a strategy and plan to achieve it. This is done by going through a formal strategic planning process. Develop a mission, vision and values statement and operational goals that map out the specific steps needed for achieving the mission. Delegate those goals to specific departments of the church. For instance, if we have an objective to create outreach programs for its community, we write actionable goals and delegate those responsibilities to individuals or teams. Then we hold them accountable for getting it done.

2. Managing Performance

The council is responsible for monitoring and holding leadership accountable for doing their job.

This is done by developing annual church goals, delegating that responsibility to leadership, and then monitoring the progress. Show support by delegating decision-making and authoritative boundaries for achieving those goals. For example, the minsters or administrators should understand the boundaries of authority for making tactical decisions about the day-today operations of the ministry. This decision-making authority removes decision bottlenecks that can hinder the progress toward achieving a goal.

3. Financial Oversight

The council oversees and ensures there is responsible stewardship of church resources, and that it maintains financial accountability, and solvency. This is done by approving and overseeing the annual church budget. Provide input and direction into strategy and prioritize spending to ensure that the strategy has the necessary financial resources to support it. Financial oversight includes identifying auditors to perform occasional audits to safeguard against embezzlement, ensure good business practices, and to maintain compliance with state and federal laws.

4. Managing Compensation

The council is responsible for compensation. This committee is responsible for leader compensation, housing allowance, and approving salaries.

5. Ensure Legal Compliance

The council is responsible for adhering to laws that govern nonprofit organizations. This includes the duties of care, loyalty, and obedience. The council has a responsibility to ensure that the church stays true to its core mission by participating in decision making, using good judgment, setting aside personal interests to ensure the best interest of the organization is kept, and by complying with governing laws.

6. Monitor Conflict-of-Interest

The council is responsible for ensuring there are no conflicts-of-interest and puts policies and systems in place to ensure full disclosure of any potential conflicts between outside organizations and church employees or the council. For instance, if a church council member owns a painting company, this could be a potential conflict if that company is given preferential treatment for outsourced painting jobs. Do this by creating a conflict-of-interest policy that requires employees and council members to disclose potential conflicts.

7. Maintain Supporting Documents and Council Records

The council is responsible for ensuring all council records are kept including:

- council minutes
- mission, vision, values statement,
- church bylaws,
- articles of incorporation
- and any policies that govern the council function.

Manage these documents by housing them on secure servers and controlled file cabinets.

8. Council Training

Help new council members by providing the appropriate orientation and training for their role. This includes a review of all corporate documents, job descriptions, and responsibilities. Also, orient them to understand the legal requirements for council members. There are many church council training resources that can help. Anyone who is chosen to be part of a church council should recognize the honor and incredible responsibility that comes with that role. Having a good understanding of role responsibilities, coupled with thorough training, is a great way to get a council member equipped to serve the church.

Biography

James Yeaw is an ordained Baptist, Interfaith and Unity Minister with degrees in Psychology and Human Resource Development from California State University. He is a graduate of Unity Institute in Missouri and holds a Doctorate in Divinity from Emerson Theological Institute. With his wife, Rev. Sharon Bush, he co-ministers to a vibrant and active congregation at Unity of Fort Collins in Colorado.

Unity Publications
Unity Publications are based on classes with Rev. Jim

These publications are a series on Unity School of Religious Studies subjects. We also have:

- *Spiritual Interpretation of the Hebrew Scriptures*
- *Spiritual Interpretation of the Christian Scriptures: The Gospels*
- *Spiritual Interpretation of the Christian Scriptures: Acts – Revelation*
- *Revelation – A Metaphysical Interpretation*
- *Unity Metaphysics*

The following book is a collection of quotations from Unity Books through 1984:

- *Quotable Quotes from Unity Books*

We have a series on the work of Classic New Thought writers. These publications include:

- *The Impersonal Life* – Joseph Benner

- *The Game of Life and How to Play It* – Florence Scovell Shinn
- *The Power of Awareness* – Neville Goddard
- *The Twelve Powers* – Charles Fillmore
- *Lessons in Truth* – H. Emilie Cady

Other books are available based on classes at Unity Spiritual Center (Arizona) and Unity of Northern Colorado. They include:
- *Christianity: A History*
- *A Country that Works for All*
- *A Course in Abundance*
- *A Course in Consciousness*
- *The Devine Feminine*
- *Discovering Unity*
- *Effective Ministry Leadership* (with Jill Campbell)
- *Perception*
- *A Practical Life with a Powerful Purpose* (with Sharon Bush)
- *Religion vs. Homosexuality*
- *A Spiritual Introduction to the World's Religions* (with Sharon Bush)
- *Thought*
- *Is Unity a Cult?*

The following is a collection of Rev. Jim's Lessons:
- *What You Seek is Seeking You*

The following publication includes a CD with a searchable database on writings from many faith traditions:
- *Wisdom of the Ages*

These publications are available on Amazon as well as Unity of Fort Collins. See additional information and other resources at our website:
www.unityfc.org

Unity Online Classes
The class presented in this book and other classes are available, without charge, on Zoom. See our website for start

dates and other information. See additional information and other resources at our website: www.unityfc.org. Rev. Yeaw is available to conduct a variety of seminars on the subjects within this book. Email: revjim@unityfc.org

Printed in Great Britain
by Amazon

43956567R00046